SORORITY GIRLS CAN CHANGE THE WORLD

Katie Mullis Bulmer

ISBN:-13:978-1542650526

Sydney,
you are a world changer.
I believe in you.
♡ Katie Bulmer
P. 64

To the hundreds of sorority women we have "adopted" over the years, this is for you.

CONTENTS

Chapter 1
Hunch Punch and Hangovers

I was once totally convinced I had found the abundant life at the best fraternity party, with the hottest date, the finest outfit, and a deliciously strong cup of hunch punch in my hand.
But when the makeup came off, the drunken buzz turned into a terrible headache, and the guy that promised forever never called again, I started to realize this life wasn't so abundant after all.

A typical sorority girl is my first language. Popularity, boys, and Bacardi was the language I learned in high school and it was tattooed upon my heart when I joined a sorority in college.

"Be skinny, wear the right makeup, get a tan, and do whatever it takes to be beautiful."

"Sleep with your boyfriend if you really like him, or just because he wants you to."

"Wear designer fashion."

"Oh, and did I mention, be beautiful?"

I am fluent in this language. It is the language I learned first. I get sorority girls and they get me. *These people are my people.*

I guess I always knew they were my girls; it just took me a while to embrace it.

God turned my life upside down during my senior year of college. I wanted to share my "upside down story" with my sorority sisters right after graduation, but there were still girls there I did keg stands with and I thought they wouldn't believe me. Then I got married, had babies, and just got busy.

As our family grew, and I grew up, I still felt this nag that I couldn't shake. I needed to share my story with sorority women.

But sorority girls are all beautiful and intimidating, and I was no longer a twenty-year-old. If this was what God wanted, He would've had to part the heavens. I would've needed to hear the plan from voice of God before I ever stepped foot on Greek Row again past graduation.

Plus, I got distracted.

I worked in youth ministry, college ministry, children's ministry, and by this point I found myself in the deep end of homeless ministry. I "saved" two women from the streets only to have one steal from me and the other push me out of her life after I helped her get a car, apartment, job, and threw a housewarming party for her to boot. I found myself exhausted and depleted. I was frustrated that the "work of Jesus" was so hard and I felt like I wasn't making any difference.

In a puddle of tears after a good ole fashioned breakdown in our walk in closet, I cried, "God, why can't I help these women?"

And then it happened.

The heavens didn't part, but they didn't have to. Never before or never since have I been so certain I heard the voice of God.

"GO SHARE YOUR STORY WITH YOUR SORORITY."

Yep, I heard the voice of God. Not in a creepy audible person next to me kind of way, but it was unmistakable. He wanted me to speak to college women, I just had to do it. After my meltdown in the closet, I finally knew God wanted me back on Greek Row. I was terrified, but one step at a time God opened all the right doors for me to go back to those beautiful mansions and tell what God had done in my life.

Fifteen years after sitting in the same chapter room, I returned to Alpha Delta Pi at Georgia Southern University as a sorority advisor. While standing in front of 225 of the most beautiful women ADPI had ever seen, I thought I was going to vomit, wet my pants, or both.

But instead, I poured my heart out…
When I was your age, like many of you, I was utterly clueless of any potential I had to "change the world" set trends, or even declare a major. My only concerns were about being pretty, popular, and attracting boys… oh my goodness boys.

Just like my sorority sisters, all the covers of Cosmopolitan magazine, and that loathsome Cinderella, I NEEDED a guy to complete me. I needed to be wanted. I needed to hear I was pretty.
I wanted the glass slipper to fit me and only me.

I was searching for my happily every after in a boyfriend. I kept thinking, "This is the guy that will bring me happiness." And every time the relationship ended I thought, "If only I was prettier, more fun, or said something different."

The parties promised to be "fun" and the guys promised we would last "forever." But most of my college days were full of hangovers, hiding, and heartbreak.

I grew up in Marietta, Georgia: a suburb of Atlanta, the buckle of the bible belt. In Atlanta, you say you're a Christian because your grandmother went to church AND you went to Vacation Bible School when you were seven.

In case that isn't proof enough of my "extreme devotion" to what I claimed I belonged, I even had a bible verse on my bulletin board in my bedroom...I know you're impressed.

Despite my awe inspiring bulletin board bible verse we weren't really a church going family.

I knew who Jesus was. I mean, I guess I did. I heard the stories about Noah, and Moses and something about death on a cross, but I didn't really get it. And I had no idea how all of these ancient stories had any application to my life.

I thought being a Christian would be a good idea…when I was a Grandma, but let's be honest Christians are a bore and I was entirely too cool for that.

Don't get me wrong, I always used the Christian card when it was convenient or I wanted someone to think I was respectable. But, for the love of being popular, there was no way I would let Jesus get in the way of having any fun. It all just seemed to costly. I knew what I had to give up and I wasn't really sure the return on the investment would be worth it.

High school and college days were full of jumping through hoops trying to be the right girl for all the wrong guys. I saw all the Nicholas Sparks movies: a pretty girl meets Ryan Gosling and they kiss passionately in the rain right after he says "you complete me." Well, maybe that was Jerry McGuire's quote but you get the idea. I was 100 percent sure a guy would bring me happily ever after. And I was 100 percent devastated every time a relationship ended.

My senior year after yet another devastating heartbreak, I came to an all time low. I tried everything in my power to find my "happily ever after," but I was always left more and more broken than before. I felt like I was desperately searching for the pieces of my broken heart, clinging to any possible hope of feeling whole again.

I felt I had nothing left of value to "ante up" in this gambling game of searching for love. My heart was not ready to even think about another boy to heal the pain. White Zinfandel helped me forget, but every morning I still woke up broken and with a headache. For 22 years I was told that a guy is what I needed for my happily ever after, but that clearly wasn't working, it never worked, and I had to find a better plan.

My friend Robin invited me to a Greek girl's bible study. I thought it was dumb and I didn't want to go. I figured all those nerdy Christian girls would be totally unrelatable, plus they could probably smell my sin and wouldn't want me to join their little club anyway. But when you're broken, you're desperate, so I figured I would give it a try.

I still remember clear as day the leader sharing with us the story of the woman at the well (John 4). She drew a picture of a cup, symbolizing the woman's desperate attempts to fill her cup with men. The cup seemed great and "full" for a moment, but what she didn't realize was that her cup was scattered with holes at the bottom. The fullness was only temporary because soon the cup would leak and become empty again.

"Everyone who drinks this water will be thirsty again, but whoever drinks the water I give them will never thirst. Indeed, the water I give them will become in them a spring of water welling up to eternal life." John 4:14, NIV

My heart stood still. I was cold and sweaty at the same time. I was thirsty, parched, and exhausted of trying to fill my heart with men. And now she was telling me there was a solution!

Eternal water…what does that even mean? But if it is true, then

PLEASE sign me up. Was it possible to feel PERMANENTLY fulfilled? Was it possible to get off the roller coaster of feeling full, then feeling completely defeated? Was there a forever that was truly forever? Eternal Water…If eternal water was on tap I wanted a keg of it.

In my apartment that night in a heap of tears and spiritual dehydration I prayed: "God I have tried every possible way I know to do things and came up empty every time. I want to try your way."

I didn't even know what that meant but God started changing me. He held my hand during the next several weeks. I surrounded myself with positive people. I stopped searching for a boyfriend and started searching to learn more about this Jesus guy who seemed so captivating with his relentless love.
All of a sudden so many things had lost their appeal. The guy who was sloppy drunk at the bar trying to pick me up seemed 100 times less attractive. The God of the universe who gave his life for a selfish party goer like me seemed 100 times more attractive. My heart was being healed by the Great Physician. The more I fell in love with my Heavenly Father, the less I needed anything else. I wasn't longing for something, I had it!

My roommate slipped a note under my door that said, "I just wanted to let you know I see the changes in you and I'm proud of you." In retrospect, I was searching for guys because I wasn't whole. I was looking to be made whole by another sinful human. Not even the best husband can do that. I had to be made whole first in Christ. Then, and only then, could I have a healthy romantic relationship.

About a year after becoming a new creation, I met this really cute youth pastor and for some reason he seemed to like me too. I had huge issues trying to understand why a youth pastor would want anything to do with me. I tried in my mind to push him away because even though I knew I was a new creation to God, how could a human look at me that way? How could this perfect guy want anything to do with someone like me?

This is where I want better for you sweet friends. I want you to meet the perfect Jesus seeking guy one day and not have to deal with telling him about your past baggage, scars from old boyfriends, and questionable party tactics. I want two complete and perfectly whole people to seek Jesus until they find each other.

I used to think following Jesus meant losing everything that was important to me.
It turns out, I found everything that was important to me.

I fell in love with my heavenly Father and he blessed me with the most amazing husband I could ever ask for. He models Christ to me on a daily basis and gives me a picture of just how much Jesus loves me.

Dear friends, I speak your language. I've been to fraternity parties hugging the toilet after too much Tequila. I've had lots of heartbreak and I've also found my happily ever after. I want to save you from tons of scars, heartbreak, and hangovers. I want to help you channel your incredible power of influence and I have some things to share that the world is simply not telling you.

Today, I am a sorority advisor. I realize that so many of us share the same story. Looking for love in all the wrong fraternity boys, which is why I wrote this book.

There are so many things I can see from this side of the fence that I just missed when I was your age. After enjoying years of college ministry, hundreds of coffee dates, and lots of marketing research, it became apparent that all women have the same basic fears, insecurities, and questions.

Sorority women have more in common than we do different. I hope for nothing more than for the words on these pages to cause you to rise up and be the change I believe to the very core of my being you can be. My prayer is something in these words will prick your heart and cause you to hear something, maybe for the first time, about the incredible world changer that you already are.

Sorority girls can…
CHANGE
THE
WORLD

I believe this to my bones.

CHAPTER 2
IT STARTS WITH TRENDS

Ah the age old question, "What is cool?"

Anyone who has been alive for more than fifteen years knows that the answer to this question changes quite frequently. In my lifetime, I was once totally convinced gaucho pants, acid washed jeans, and *New Kids On the Block* were the cooler than a polar bear's toenail.

But at some point my acid washed jeans were in a garage sale and my *New Kids On the Block* cassette tapes (they are a thing) were in the trash.

I've studied marketing for as long as I can remember. I was a marketing major with an emphasis in sales. I've worked in print, radio, and TV advertising firms in New York City, Atlanta, and a few small towns in Georgia.

Currently, I work with apparel and print marketing, primarily selling bulk orders of 100+ T-shirts to universities and organizations. In this industry, I get the updates and the first wind of the next "great thing."

I get paid to track when something is cool or lame and the money that changes hands in the meantime. All this trend studying and experience brings me to one unmistakable conclusion:

Sorority girls can
CHANGE
THE
WORLD

$100 Million Dollar Influence

Comfort Colors, the T-shirt brand, was founded in 1975. For years it was popular in beach shops along the coast. When I first started in the apparel industry, none of the sorority t-shirt chains I worked with had ever heard of Comfort Colors tees. I saw them at a few trade shows, but I rarely had any customers ask for them. At the time, sorority girls liked fitted tees and usually ordered the smallest size they could wear. Yet, the T-shirt industry was about to be totally flipped on it's head, thanks to sorority girls.

No one knows where or why, but around 2010, sorority girls decided they liked Comfort Colors oversized tees. Almost overnight, sales of Comfort Colors exploded in popularity. I received updates on a weekly basis notifying us of stock shortages as Comfort Colors scrambled to keep up with demand. The small sizes were ordered less and the larger sizes were produced in abundance as the fad shifted to oversized tees. Annual sales of Comfort Colors tees skyrocketed from $10 million to $100 million dollars[1]!

The crazy thing is the sudden peak in demand was not due to any extra marketing or promotion from the company.

---

[1] http://directdesigninc.com/comfort-colors/

Sorority girls simply decided they liked Comfort Colors, posted about them on social media, and wore them all the time. Without any extra marketing dollars, Comfort Colors grew ten fold! This is an entrepreneur's dream!

The sudden love affair with the oversized tee also birthed the Spirit football jersey craze with the sorority letters written across the shoulders. The trend looked so good on Greek Row, that high school girls wanted them too. Today, even our small company gets orders for these custom jerseys from day cares, gyms, and even church groups, while our industry makes thousands of dollars in the process.

THANK YOU SORORITY GIRLS!

I have seen the same thing happen with black rimmed glasses, yoga pants, the messy bun, and whatever the fascination is with pineapples. What was once considered nerdy, sloppy, or irrelevant turns into a multi-million-dollar business when sorority girls decide it's cool.

With such incredible trend setting potential and millions of dollars hanging in the balance, this phenomenon of "what is cool" has been studied by many marketers and economists.

Malcom Gladwell, author and social sciences researcher is arguably an expert in this arena. In his book, *The Tipping Point*, Gladwell explains these huge marketing successes as "The Law of the Few."

"The Law of the Few" supports the idea that "the success of any kind of social epidemic is heavily dependent on the involvement of people with a particular and rare set of social gifts.[2] In other words, when trends shift, the few people with "a rare set of social gifts" are the ones riding the first wave of "cool," while the rest of the world follows.

Never has "The Law of the Few" been more applicable than with sorority girls. What they wear, where they eat, and what they get tattooed (seriously) gets noticed and shifts the mainstream culture.

Sororities are filled with popular girls, who organically socialize with other popular people, have large social networks, and can make what was once an almost unheard of brand of t-shirts sell for 10 million dollars.

Sorority women also have on average 50 percent more followers on social media than their non Greek peers. With any given post, sorority women can influence their social platform of thousands of people.
Even the least friendly of the bunch is placed in an environment to effortlessly meet tons of people and socialize with the most influential students on campus. Even if they aren't cool, their friends are…therefore they are.

The few cool kids that set trends are also equipped with the largest social network among their peers. This is the perfect recipe to turn even the ugliest of fads back into style.

But don't take my word for it. *The Fraternity Advisor*[3] has some

---

2
https://malcolmgladwelltippingpoint.wikispaces.com/The+Law+of+the+Few
[3] http://thefraternityadvisor.com/greek-life-statistics/

incredible research on the world changers that are sorority girls.

Over 85 percent of the student leaders on some 730 campuses are involved in the Greek community.

The first Female Senator was Greek.

The first Female Astronaut was Greek.

All of the Apollo 11 Astronauts are Greek.

Over $7 million is raised each year by Greeks nationally.

850,000 hours are volunteered by Greeks annually.

71 percent of those listed in "Who's Who in America" belong to a sorority or fraternity.

This is a remarkable power of influence. Look at these incredible statistics! If that isn't proof you can change the world, I don't know what is! I could end the book here, but I'm going to talk about sex in the next chapter so you probably want to stay tuned.

What if this incredible leadership potential was channeled in the right direction? What would happen if this unique trend setting potential started movements that made a difference?

It could…

CHANGE
THE
WORLD

WHO IS IN CHARGE HERE?

I hope I have made my point clear that sorority women can make anything in vogue.

I see it happen all the time. Marketers and advertisers understand your power of influence and they want your dollars.

You are the hottest consumer demographic in America. At 33 million strong with an estimated worth of $150 billion dollars, marketers care a great deal about what attracts you and what "it" thing you fall in love with next.

In the documentary titled *Merchants of Cool*, [4] marketers, experts, and economists explore the relationship between the media and you. The remarkable thing is you each look to each other for identity. You probably never thought about the media and apparel industry looking to you for what is cool just as much or more than you look to them, but it is true.

The 60-year-old bald and overweight media executive in his high rise office needs the "next big thing" to drive profits, but he is clueless as to what is cool. So, his team conducts focus groups and surveys asking you, their target market, what is indeed cool?

When it comes to movies, TV shows, radio, or pretty much any other media, did you know only 232 media executives control the information diet of 277 million Americans? That's one media exec to

---

[4] http://www.pbs.org/wgbh/pages/frontline/shows/cool/view/

850,000 subscribers. [5]

Believe it or not, in the U.S. there are just six corporations that control 90 percent of what we read, watch, or listen to. Due to mergers, buyouts, etc., the 50+ companies that ruled the airways back in 1983 have consolidated into just six

The 232 media execs in their fancy Hollywood office, far removed from your actual life, are simply looking to get rich and don't have your best interest at heart. No offense to the media makers, I was one after all. Nevertheless, I have yet to sit in a boardroom where there was a discussion on how to convey healthy relationships, model positive friendships, or have a girl put on *more* clothing.

Generally speaking, the media doesn't care if a movie encourages you to go and have too much sex or act irresponsibly, they just want you to download the music, buy the tickets, wear the T-shirts, and watch the DVDs.

It's Not Even Real

My husband and I recently went on a trip to Las Vegas, Nevada. He had a work conference and I was able to come along to enjoy the city. It took us about five minutes from getting off the airplane to realize Sin City lives up to it's name. Billboards, signs, and lights, advertising sex EVERYWHERE. Nearly nude women everywhere who "want to meet you" so the billboard reads. The streets were littered with little cards of nude women. Every casino smelled like

---

5

http://www.businessinsider.com/these-6-corporations-control-90-of-the-media-in-a merica-2012-6 cigarettes, booze, and regrets.

Yet even with all of this, what struck me about Vegas was the huge beautifully ornate and strikingly elaborate hotels full of amenities fit for royalty. Shows full of talent were matched by none other. The streets, full of lights and glamour, lit up with breathtaking beauty under the night sky. Exquisite detail went into every inch of the architecture.

One morning, while waiting for the elevator, I stood astonished at the elaborate oil paintings, Persian rugs, and lavish decor from floor to ceiling. My eyes followed the seam of the intricate wood finish on the side of the elevator. That's when I noticed the veneer that was peeling off at the corner. What looked like 1,000 year old wood pulled fresh from some exotic forest was actually a cheap covering. It wasn't even real. What looked to be alluring and beautiful was just an inexpensive mask.

Staring at that wall, I felt that was the perfect example of the media. We don't really stop to think about it, but we personalize and try to relate to the shows and movies that we know are fiction. That's human nature. That's normal and even healthy. The big screen has been captivating us for years, motivating, inspiring, and letting us fall in love with love all over again.

But it's not even real.
We have allowed media to teach us what is right and acceptable yet the people making these movies and shows are simply trying to make money. Your future, your well being and your heart is NOT even considered in making the script.

The conclusion? "Kids feel frustrated and lonely today because they are encouraged to feel that way," Mark Miller states in *Merchants of Cool.* " Miller continues...

Advertising has always sold anxiety and it certainly sells anxiety to the young. It's always telling them that they are not thin enough, they're not pretty enough, they don't have the right friends, or they have no friends...they're losers unless they're cool. But I don't think anybody, deep down, really feels cool enough, ever."

So here's my question...

If you sorority girls, maintain such an incredible power of influence that you can grow an average t-shirt company to a 100-million-dollar business, and even make a pineapple all the rage, why in the name of cute shoes would you let *MTV*, *The Bachelor*, *Cosmopolitan*, or 232 money hungry strangers with an agenda have any say whatsoever over your one extraordinary and precious life?

You are the coolest trendsetters the world has ever known! You decide what is acceptable, you decide what you pour into that beautiful mind of yours, and you decide where to spend your dollars. You are smarter than the commercials, *The Gilmore Girls*, and the hype. You are the hype!

Be the change you want to see.

Your Dollars Matter

I bet you didn't know you could change the world with a cup of coffee. The coffee industry is very corrupt. Many farmers are forced into poverty because they are not paid fairly for the coffee beans they grow. The $5 latte bought at retail may only earn a farmer as low as $.02. Co-ops, exporters, importers, storage facilities, roasters, and the coffee shop all get a portion of that $5 cup. What percentage goes where is not always fair. Often it is the farmers who have the most back breaking work, but gets paid the least.

However, many fair trade organizations are looking to end this disproportion of funds.

Three Tree Coffee is a local coffee shop in my neck of the woods. A young couple started the shop with a roaster and a dream to make a difference. They decided before the first cup was sold, they would ensure farmers and everyone else involved from farm to cup, were paid fairly. The farmers, where *Three Tree Coffee* beans are grown, are able to provide for their families, earn a living, and even invest back into their crop, therefore making a better bean in the long run.

This little missional coffee shop is not only changing the world for farmers. In a year end letter from 2016, owner Philip Klayman took a look back at their impact:

"In 2016, we paid $2,669.77 MORE to coffee farmers than industry standard! We mean it when we say our coffee was not produced through any form of slave labor!

We raised $948 for women in Zimbabwe, simply by selling their products in our store. These women have AIDS and are widowed, resulting in them not having a trajectory for success in their culture. We are helping by giving them a market.
We raised $329.69 for Out of Darkness, a ministry that rescues and restores victims of sex
trafficking in Atlanta, through fundraiser events.

We raised $210 for True Justice International's safe house construction through similar fundraising events.

We raised $294.50 for a building project in Ethiopia through Go Design by donating $0.50 of
every Ethiopian retail bag we sell. Similarly, we raised $30.50 for Safe Haven, a domestic violence, by donating $0.50 of every Rwandan retail bag we sell.

We hosted many spirit/percentage nights, helping local organizations raise a total of $608.52
for charities of their choice. We participated in 2 auctions raising $1,036.65 for Café Femenino and Grounds for Health. Both organizations fund programs to empower coffee farmers."

Total Ethical Impact = $6,127.63

And you thought you were just buying a cappuccino.

Sorority girls found out about *Three Tree Coffee*, and I bet you know what happened next. The company grew...like a lot, which is incredible because at *Three Tree Coffee* not only are you buying a cup of coffee, you are ending poverty and freeing slaves.

And this is my point.

With every purchase we make we are supporting the factory where it was made, the importer, exporter, the distributor, and many marketers along the way.

What if the world's trendsetters decided, for example, purses made by artisans freed from slavery were the next big thing? Could you imagine the global impact that could have?

I get that this may be a totally new concept to you so don't get overwhelmed. I am simply trying to make the point that sorority women have incredible power to start trends. I am merely asking you to consider starting trends with a more far reaching impact than making a pineapple cool.

If you don't know where to start, there's an app for that! The "Ethical Barcode" lets you scan almost any barcode and rates the product according to health, environment, and social impact. Also projectjust.com[6] is a website where you can search the brands you love and understand the ethics behind it.

But the best way to change the world is to start small. Maybe there is a local cause or boutique near your campus doing great things in your community or around the world. Your sorority can host a spirit night supporting the local shop, promote the tastiest thing on their menu, and wear their T-shirts. When sorority girls support moral organizations, they sell more. When they sell more, they can better support their honest practices and set a higher bar for the competition..Eventually changing the world.

---

[6] http://projectjust.com/

Faith is not accepting the world as it is, but insisting on building the world God wants. - Shane Claiborne

Buy the coffee that supports fair trade, buy the purses made sold through amazing organizations like Ten Thousand Villages[7], and spend your dollars where you can make a lasting impact.

Tell marketers what you support with your dollars. Your trendsetting potential to support ethical companies, movies with a positive message, and uplifting music could entirely…
CHANGE
THE
WORLD.

---

[7] http://www.tenthousandvillages.com/

World Changing Action Steps

1. Is any of the above information a shocker to you? Were you aware of your power of influence?

2. Vote with your dollars. Tell companies what you want to see more.
"Plugged in" is a great app that rates movies and "ethical barcode" is an app where you can scan barcodes to ensure the product you are buying doesn't support sweatshops or slave labor.

3. What is something positive your sorority could make the "next big trend?"

Chapter 3
Sex and Greek row

If true love could be found at 18, then we had found it. He was fiercely handsome. We were completely infatuated with each other. He would write down all the lyrics to love songs and mail them to me. (Gag. I know, but at the time I thought it was so romantic).

There was no such thing as too much time together. We had it bad for each other. Passion mixed with hormones and no strong enough reason to abstain, led us to sleep together." And as a result, my heart was my ever more glued to his. But it was fine because we would be forever. All our friends said we would stand the test of time and I mean who better to trust than your seventeen year old peers?

He moved away to college and we were good at first, the long distance thing was fine. But, when he came back home to take me to my senior prom I knew something wasn't right.

As he put the car into park after driving me home that night, he began his speech. Something about how he will always love me, but we both need to "spread our wings" and he doesn't want to "hold me back." And this wasn't really a break up on the night of my senior prom…it was just taking a "step back."

But all I could hear was the outright crumbling of my heart. I declined his offer to walk me to the door so I could get inside as soon as possible to totally become unglued.

It was after midnight. The house was quiet so I stuffed my face in my pillow and sobbed. If crying so hard could kill you, I was pretty sure I would have died that night.

It is heartbreak. It is real. It is devastating, and it is made infinitely more complicated by this thing we call sex.

Our culture has confused it, depreciated it, abused it, and hasn't done a thing to make it a bit easier in this already complicated world. I know navigating this dating world is not easy. I learned a lot the hard way.

If you get nothing else from this book I pray you get something from this chapter on sex. There is no erase button on the decisions we make with our bodies. But no one tells you this when you are 18.

YOU DECIDE

When I speak at sorority houses, I love to do this little exercise with them. I bring a small dry erase board and ask them to shout out characteristics they want in their dream husband. I am clear that I want them to think long term here. So yes, a cute guy is clearly important, but I also want to hear what values they will cherish when they are raising teenagers, dealing with losing family members, or money stress. What characteristics describe the LIFE PARTNER you want beside you?

Here is a list of the most common adjectives I hear:

Smart
Funny
Cute (duh)
Christian leader
Wants to raise our kids in church
Healthy/Fit
Faithful
Doesn't sleep around
Has manners
Nice to his Mama
Goal setter
Ambitious
Friendly

Not a surprising list. We all really want the same basic things in our prince charming. The kicker lies when I ask the hard question: Why in the world would the most beautiful women on campus accept anything less than what we see on this list?

I have met women in every sorority and I have yet to hear a girl say they want their dream guy to pretend to love them, say all the right things, use their body, and then never call them again.
Yet, I have had coffee with entirely too many girls as they sip their latte in tears and share their confusion over a guy who seemed to really like them, but after sex won't even talk to them in class the next week.

Here's the thing no one told you, sweet friend. Take a deep breath and inhale every word I say next…

You decide what is acceptable in the guy you date.

Just as in trends, movies, and t-shirts, you decide what is acceptable, not the media and not the guy. You play off of each other. If you flirt with a guy you know you shouldn't flirt with, he will pursue you (did I mention that sorority girls are beautiful?). If you say it's okay to go back to his apartment after too many Jell-O shots, he thinks it's okay to kiss. If you say it's fine to lay on his bed, he is not an idiot.

Does this sound like the book *If You Give a Mouse a Cookie?* You decide where you want to draw the line and I suggest putting the line 2 steps behind the actual line you want to cross. This is why we have guardrails on the highway. You don't want to touch a guardrail, but you really don't want to fall into a ditch.

Marinate on this for a minute. Does the guy you are dating now or have recently dated know what you define as acceptable and not? Have you taken the time to determine what is important to you in a guy and what lines you don't want to cross? Do you want to look back on your college days and say you slept with as many men as you possibly could, or do you want to walk down the isle one day and give your heart, body, and whole self over to be completely honored, respected, and intimately known by a man who loves you too much to put you in a compromising position before the "I do's?"

YOU MUST BE WILLING TO WALK AWAY

The Huffington Post[8] wrote an exceptional article explaining our current dating culture in simple economic terms:

"It's a question of supply and demand. "Easy" women are easy to get. The supply exceeds the demand. Now, it's the sexually modest woman that stands apart in the dating world as a rare and desirable thing.

Rare and Desirable. I like these adjectives. What woman wouldn't want someone to describe her as rare and desirable? Yet many mislead sorority women still believe that the way to get a man's attention is to dress with their boobs hanging out and wear skirts that are no bigger than a napkin while dancing on a table and doing body shots. Does this describe rare and desirable?

Ladies, if you're not sitting down yet you may want to for this next part. This is straight from the lips of men and may rattle to the core what you thought you knew about guys.

From the *Good Man Project*[9] (a hugely popular online magazine for guys) puts it like this:

Ladies, if you really want men to step up and become the real men you talk about, you must demand it. I'm not saying ask for it, I'm not saying hope for it, I'm saying demand it. What does that mean? It means you don't settle for anything less. It means if you aren't

---

[8] http://www.huffingtonpost.ca/debra-macleod/2015-dating_b_6385346.html
[9] https://goodmenproject.com/featured-content/the-good-life-ladi es-demand-what-you-want/

satisfied, you walk away. Men will rise up and meet your challenge, I promise, it's what we do best. We love challenges. We love it when women make us step up and work.

If you do this right, you will have men lining up at your door. It seems counter-intuitive, but you have to understand how much men enjoy challenge. There is nothing sexier than a woman who has the confidence to call us out and challenge us to rise up. The part that you don't like is the hardest thing about all this. You must be willing you walk away if you aren't getting what you want. I will say this five more times because it's that important.

You must be willing to walk away

You must be willing to walk away

You must be willing to walk away.

You must be willing to walk away.

You must be willing to walk away.

DROPS THE MIC.

This truth has never been more applicable for sorority women. Ladies, look in the mirror. Not only are you the most striking women on your campus, but you are almost always an all around "good catch." Like the statics from the last chapter proved, sorority women are typically involved on campus, earn good grades, are responsible, come from nice families, and have good manners as a bonus.

Why in the world are the most amazing women in the world settling for anything less than the characteristics they put on their "ideal list?"

WHAT IF I NEVER GET MARRIED?

Maybe you're thinking, that list is a good idea in theory, but good grief Katie, what if I never get married? What if this narrows my dating pool?

Girlfriend, let's be real for a second. I get it. I was the girl who pretended I was strong and independent, but if I were to be honest, I would do whatever it took to make my boyfriend happy, anything to avoid another broken heart. I thought if I didn't settle for close to best, or overlook a few flaws then I was going to end up being alone. I was utterly terrified to be a middle aged woman with jelly donuts and 17 cats as my only companions.

Now that I'm married with kiddos (no cats) and have a little life under my belt, I see this question much differently. I look across our lattes as we sit together at the coffee shop listening to the nineteen-year-old worried she won't find a husband. With the same genuine love that I showed her because I totally remember feeling that way at 19, I look at you now and honestly want to say, "You are an infant! I can still smell the Similac on your breath! What in the actual heck are you worried about?"

Good news from my side of the fence:
Do you know how many of my sorority sisters, friends from college, or other acquaintances did NOT get married?
Two. As in 1 more than 1. As in only 2.

I don't know how to prove what kind of odds that is other than comparing it with how many people I currently know on Facebook.

Assuming we know about the same amount of people that gives you a .0016 chance that you won't get married. The odds are in your favor.

While I only have 2 friends that never married, I know tons of people who are fighting custody battles with their kids because they are divorced or married and miserable. Permission to speak freely here?

While there are few guarantees in the marriage and dating world, I do have one guarantee for you: Sleep with as many men as you want, give your heart, and body away with little or no expectations and I guarantee you will have a million and 1 marriage problems, if marriage works out at all.

Yikes I know, I said it.

OR

You can be different than the world by protecting your heart and body. You can work on becoming the best future wife you can be with as little baggage to carry into the marriage as possible.

Worry less about getting married and more about becoming a whole, complete, loved by Jesus you. Wouldn't you want your future husband to be doing the same thing?

34

Having unshakable standards WILL narrow your dating pool. The guys that think dating you is optional, sex is a game to be played, and are sloppy drunks will no longer be considered as feasible options for you. Your dating pool is now smaller, you're welcome.

Are You the Person You Are Looking For Is Looking For?

Here's the other kicker in my little dry-erase-board-prince-charming-exercise. It's easy to come up with a list of qualities we want in our dream guy but what if we turn the tables? Does this list of ideal characteristics describe you?

Andy Stanley in his series, *Love, Sex and Dating*[10] (go watch it on YouTube right now) asks this now famous question to thousands of singles. "Are you the person you are looking for, is looking for?"

In high school and most of college I was not. I had my list of what Prince Charming would look like, but I figured in the meantime I could dance on tables, get really drunk, and give my heart and body away to any guy that said all the right things. I realize now how hypocritical I was in wanting my dream guy to protect his body and mind, love Jesus, and be debt-free. Being devilishly handsome would

---

10

http://northpoint.org/messages/the-new-rules-for-love-sex-and-dating

also be a nice bonus.

All the while I assumed I could do as I pleased and expect my dream guy to pursue me?

How did this ever make sense to me? And how does this still make sense in the mind of singles everyday? This whole idea hit home for me in a grocery store check out line.

When my husband and I were just friends, we were working together on a church project and needed to run to the grocery store. We were standing together at the checkout line when he grabbed a *Cosmopolitan Magazine*, which as usual, paraded a beautiful half nude woman and included a ton of articles featuring something about sex.

You can imagine my nervousness at first as he grabbed the magazine. But he did something strange, something I had never seen done before. As quickly as he grabbed it, he turned the magazine backwards and then set it back on the stand. Then, he looked back at me and proceeded with our conversation as if it was a totally normal thing to do.

Dumbfounded and confused, I said, "Why did you do that…that thing with the magazine?"

Casually, with a shrug he replied, "Oh, to protect my eyes. I just don't want fake images in my mind to compare my wife to one day."

Let's all take a moment to *swoon.* He had me at "protect my eyes."

As I found out more about this totally weird (in a really good way) guy, I also realized he had programs on his computer to protect him from internet porn. He even asked himself questions like, "Would I be comfortable bringing everything I watched, listened to, or read to church with me on Sunday?" Maybe he was in some twelve step recovery program, I thought? Nope, it turns out he just learned a valuable lesson early in life:

It is much easier to avoid temptation than to overcome it.

Who was this guy and where had he been all my life?

Eager to tell my friends about this new guy, I specifically remember having the conversation with one of my dear friends, Amanda. She is beautiful. Likely one of my most beautiful friends. She was popular, smart, and had no problem attracting boyfriends. But, like most of my sorority girlfriends, she liked to party, hook up with guys, and place Jesus in a convenient little box, careful not to let Him get in the way of her having fun.

When I shared the grocery store story with her, she seemed spellbound but also totally in love with the idea that there were guys out there like this. She decided she was worthy of a guy who mirrored those qualities and with determination she told me, "I'm going to marry a guy like that."

I don't know why I was so surprised to hear her say that. In fact, most of my friends who heard about this guy "protecting his eyes for his future spouse" all had their hearts flutter like a teenage girl at a One Direction concert.

I didn't know how to respond to Amanda when she told of her genuine desire to have all these qualities in her Mr. Right, while spending no time becoming Mrs. Right. No matter how beautiful or talented she is, guys like that are looking for a lady that is traveling in the same direction. The type of guy that is protecting his eyes and body while wholeheartedly pursuing Christ is not looking for the girl at the bar with tons of sexual experiences under her belt.

It's like Amanda was headed east and her dream Christian man was headed west and she somehow thought they would meet up in the same place and live happily every after with sunshine and rainbows.

I don't know why I didn't see it earlier. I was the exact same way just a few months before we had this very conversation. I had recently become a Christian and Jesus had just pulled a total 180 on my life. I too dreamed of marrying a kind man who would love me just as Christ loved the church. I dreamed of him protecting me and being the spiritual leader of our family one day. Yet, a few months before I met Bryan, I was simply not the type of girl he would have liked.

The pursuit of a romance to make all your dreams come true is not only impossible, but also totally unfair to put that burden on another sinful human being.

  Jesus is the only one who can truly fulfill you. Your boyfriend is not your savior, and you are not his.

I think the real question is not "Will I get married?" but "Is my God big enough to take care of this?"

He is a good father. He sees you begging and pleading for what you think will fulfill your heart. But, he loves you too much to let you believe the lie that another human can fill the void that only He can fill. He wants to pour into your broken places to make you whole and complete. He wants you to become the person who you are looking for is looking for, not just for them, but for yourself as well. Enjoy your single time. Make the most of it. And don't worry. God's got this.

Change Your Focus

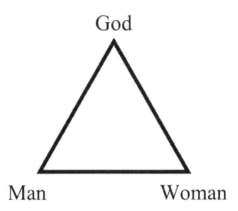

This is how the whole male-female relationship is supposed to work. The woman keeps her eye on the prize of closeness with her creator and worries 100x less about what guys think of her. She is fully confident that her future is in the strong and capable hands of a Creator who has every detail of her life already under control.

The men get to do what they do best: run, peruse, and sweat their way through temptation and lesser definitions of "fun," also with their eyes on the prize.

Both are becoming whole, both are getting rid of baggage, and both are learning more and more about how to love because of the one who loved them first.

At the top of the triangle, an amazing girl and guy who have been fighting the good fight together, meet. Oh my goodness, Nicholas Sparks has nothing on the type of romance that can begin here. This is what we dream of.

Please friends if you hear nothing else, listen carefully to this, fifteen years later I have approximately zero friends who wish they would have had more sex when they were in college. It turns out there is no erase button to a sexual encounter. The decisions you make today with your body, will be with you the rest of your life.

Stop chasing boys and start chasing Jesus. It could
CHANGE
THE
DATING
WORLD
… and it will most definitely change your world.

World Changing Action Steps

1. Make a list detailing what describes your dream guy. Turn the list on yourself and become the dream girl.

2. As my husband learned much earlier than me, temptation is easier to avoid than overcome. What is a way you can put yourself in less tempting situations?

3. What relationship do you have to honestly, and painfully be willing to just WALK AWAY.

CHAPTER 4
PHILANTHROPY

I hope you had a tall glass of ice water after all that sex talk. And I hope you are sitting down. I have another idea that will totally blow your hair back.

First let's state what sororities are totally doing right here. Every sorority has a philanthropy. The organizations they choose benefits in big ways from the generous events and fundraisers done by sororities. Collectively, each sorority donates millions of dollars to amazing charities worldwide every year. This is world changing!

But I believe sorority girls are more amazing than one philanthropy. I believe sorority women have the potential to turn the city where they call their college home into the best city on the planet AND send members to the most forgotten places on the globe to share their world changing power there as well.
Currently the social budget is on average four times that of the philanthropy. Socials are fun, and I'm a big believer in always having fun.

BUT, what if (I hope you're sitting down for this. Take a deep breath) philanthropy was more important than socials? Or better yet, what if philanthropy was the social?

Breath into a brown paper bag…I promise it will be fun.

Imagine if 150 girls partnered with a fraternity (which is what you do a lot anyway) and brought all of that man (and woman) power to Habitat for Humanity or any other local organization dedicated to changing the community? That is 300 young, able, and excited workers coming together to build a house, paint a building, play with kids, or clean up the city! What if all 300 guys and girls saved the $5 they would normally spend on just one drink and donated it to said organization? That's $1,500! That could go a long way for a non-profit.

Alpha Delta Pi at Georgia Southern University took this idea and ran with it. One Saturday, they divided up their chapter of 225 girls and invested into the community. Girls split up into groups. Throughout the community, sorority women were spending time with our local nursing home residents, helping with a pet adoption, teaching children in the community about sustainability, painting a floor for a fostering agency, volunteering for upwards soccer, and building a gardening bed for the STEM classroom at a low income school.

The dollars that would have normally gone to this "social" were invested into the community. They were able to write checks and buy supplies that made the community blubber in appreciation.

"Service Social," as it was called, served the city in a big way. It gave community leaders a different view of sorority women. Their involvement made the local paper and is still making a difference months later. It's amazing the impact a group of girls could make on one day in just a few hours.

GSU Alpha Delta Pi community service chair, Anna Jeffords said it this way, "Serving the community has given me a drive to make even bigger service opportunities happen for others during my lifetime. It's so easy to get caught up as a college student with school, your social life, and other stressors- I didn't expect service alongside my friends could bring my heart so much contentment!"

This is re-defining fun. This is fun on a whole new level. Just like Anna said, her heart was so content from serving.

Brandon Hatmaker, pastor of Austin New Church, author, and world changer has an interesting observation about groups serving the community in his book, *Interrupted.* Mr. Hatmaker states, "Community Groups structured mainly for the benefit of their members have about a three year shelf life. They lose interest after this point because they get bored and discontent."

Ever notice that the seniors are significantly less involved than the freshman? Seniors simply start to wonder how often they can go to the same functions and watch the same girls cry over boys and get sick in the bathroom. Hatmaker would argue this discontentment is due to a lack of serving within the community.

"We have an innate craving to live on mission with God in this dangerous, and exciting world. Out there is where we come to life, and get over ourselves." -Brandon Hatmaker

---

We are simply wired to serve.

Sure it's easier and more comfortable to stay clean and serve just ourselves, but something within us wants more.

We crave a lasting impact. We want to make a difference in the world around us. We want to
CHANGE
THE
WORLD.

Imagine the impact on the community if a sorority brought this world changing power on a regular basis. Imagine the cleaner cities, better equipped charities, and projects completed faster all around your city thanks to you, sorority girls.

Not only would the community benefit, but you would too. Serving is apart of our DNA. Our hearts are content when we see the look on a senior citizen's face after a long visit, or a child who has a chance to play in a clean inner city park. We are happiest when our head hits the pillow after a long day of building homes for the homeless and painting over graffiti. I have never seen sorority girls more beautiful than with dirty hands and tired feet.

"Never doubt that a small group of thoughtful, committed citizens can change the world; indeed, it's the only thing that ever has."
-Margaret Mead

Can you say that about your last social?

If your sorority lost its charter tomorrow, who in the city would miss you? Would the organizations in your city that are making a difference miss your partnership or would the bars miss your business on Tequila Tuesdays? What lasts longer? What makes a greater impact? What will you remember when you are thirty (hint…you definitely won't remember Tequila Tuesday).

If sororities looked to who is making a difference in their community and asked, "How can we help?", this would totally *change the world.* Who can make this happen? You! I am sure at least some of you reading these words are the social, philanthropy, or community service chair that can start planning this today. If you're not, I bet you know her number. Send this chapter to her and start making plans.

Contact your local alumni to ask them for contacts in the community. It may turn out that our Greek alumni are world changers too. Chances are, you have several local alumni in service organizations that would be delighted to have the assistance from your chapter! Even in the small town of Statesboro, Georgia, alumni were able to help Georgia Southern sororities reach out to several world changing organizations. I am sure your chapter could do the same.

If you still need ideas check out womenworldchangers.org.

Remember you are a trend setter, you are a connector, and one of the few who can decide that something needs to be different. A movement will happen. If you are afraid, it's okay. All great leaders are afraid. The thing that sets you apart is your willingness to keep moving with your fear. Where there is fear, there is an opportunity for leadership.

Would you rather be remembered as the girl who lead her sorority to help thousands of homeless children, rebuilt a retirement center, and cleaned up the inner city, or the girl who was an expert at keg stands? You decide your legacy, choose wisely.

WORLD CHANGING ACTION STEPS

1. Discuss this idea of a "service social" with a few sisters and bring it to your exec. board.

2. Ask a local alumnus if they can recommend a great organization that could use the help of your sorority. If you can't get the whole chapter on board, maybe your pledge class or group of friends can start the "trend."

3. Ask the philanthropy chair how the chapter can better help serve your philanthropy and make this year your most generous year ever!

Chapter 5
Sisterhood

Have you ever thought about why you joined your sorority? I'm sure you have compelling reasons about the sisters, the reputation, and the impressive pref day song, but I bet you never realized you were actually *created* for community.

Community is something we all want. No matter how you're wired, social butterfly or socially awkward, something in your soul longs for meaningful relationships with others. We treasure friendships that allow us to truly "be ourselves." All of us long for a deep, authentic, and genuine community.

Dr. Brené Brown[11], author, researcher, and extremely popular TED talk speaker, has become well known for her research on vulnerability, courage, worthiness, and shame. After years of research, one of her surprising discoveries were "connection is what gives purpose and meaning to our lives. This is what we are all about."

The truth is, we need each other. God gave us each other to walk alongside, encourage, and spur one another on. We all crave to belong. Even Tom Hanks had "Wilson" in the ever popular movie *Cast Away*. We need other people. It's our lifeblood!

---

[11] http://brenebrown.com/

Show me your friends, and I'll show you your future.

"If you want to see your life in five years take the average of the people with whom you spend the most time." - Jim Rohn

Who you hang out with is one of the biggest influencers on your decisions and predictors of your future. Your peers have the ability to influence your major, who you date, and even where you move after graduation. In my own life, if it wasn't for my friend Stephanie, I never would have gone to Georgia Southern University. If not for my friend April, I never would have moved to NYC after graduation. And if not for my friend Katie, I never would have met my husband.

Who you hang out with matters a great deal. It's time to ask some hard questions about who you surround yourself with. What friends live a life you admire? Do you make questionable decisions when you hang out with a certain group? How can you surround yourself with uplifting friends? How can you be an uplifting friend yourself?

THE POWER OF SISTERS

Our good friends, Christa and Luke, had three little girls, but their family was not yet complete. Christa and Luke went through the adoption process to bring home a precious three-year-old girl from China named Sadie. Sadie has Down syndrome and spent the first three years of her life rarely leaving her crib. The staff at the orphanage believed Sadie was not capable of smiling, walking, or talking. Sadie was almost never held, spoken to, and didn't have opportunity to develop her muscles. At three-years-old she could not yet crawl.

But then, Sadie came to her new home and met her new sisters (at the time) ages five, four, and two. Sadie's new sisters didn't see Down syndrome; they didn't see weak muscles. They saw a new friend and sister!

Christa and Luke were naturally cautious and unsure about how much Sadie could learn and how quickly, but not her sisters. They said "let's go play!" It was just a few months before Sadie's muscles got stronger. It wasn't long before Sadie was crawling around to follow her sisters as they played. A child they were told would never smile, soon learned to belly laugh.

One day while Christa was cooking, she nearly fell over in shock as she saw the oldest sister walking down the hall with Sadie, who was taking steps for the very first time. "Go Sadie go," they shouted. Her sisters only a hair bigger than Sadie were cheering her along the sidelines as she took her first steps.

Now, Sadie has been in her new family for almost two years. She has grown leaps and bounds. Would she have made progress in a loving family versus an orphanage? Of course. But it's obvious to see that her sisters have been some of her biggest cheerleaders. They never saw weakness in Sadie, but always gave her the confidence she needed to grow stronger.

Imagine a friendship, a sisterhood like Sadie and her sisters. Imagine friends that don't see your weakness, but instead sees a friend and won't let you settle for anything less than your best. When you're beaten down by the world, buried in self doubt, insecurity, and have just given up, your sisters won't take your defeat as an option. They know you're a fighter, and they won't let you rest until you are the best version of yourself! This is sisterhood at it's best!

I HAVE A DREAM OF SISTERHOOD

I have a dream of ideal friendships where you are loved not in spite of your flaws, but loved even more because of them. I dream of a kind of friendship where you are inspired to be the best your friends already believe you are.

I wish for you friends that don't simply agree if you're making poor choices, but lovingly tell you the truth you need to hear.
I wish for you friends that see the potential in you and never let you settle for status quo. Just as iron sharpens iron, I pray your friends love you so much you can't help but grow into the world changers they see in you.

I pray for a friend that lovingly hugs you when you realize that guy is not God's best for you. I wish for you, friendships so genuine and brave, your friends won't let you go out with another guy until you realize your identity in Christ. May your dear friends challenge you to become whole and complete, learning truly what love is before you try to give or receive love from another.

I pray for friends that tell you when you have stuff in your teeth,
laugh at your jokes, and encourage you to be brave.
May you light the way on this road less traveled becoming a young
woman after God's own heart.

More than I wish you have this type of friend, I pray you are one.

Dear sorority friends, this is true sisterhood and the dream of all your founding members. Friendships like this are rare, beautiful, and the kind that spur each other onto world changing potential. Friendships like these are not easily found unless they're made, on purpose.

This sisterhood is really the match to the explosion I see happening on Greek Row.

Sisterhood is the only way you can stay strong enough to paddle through
the ocean full of temptation out there. You need each other huddled
together in the barracks of the war over your heart.

After fighting the battles, you come back to your sisters to heal your wounds. Their words of encouragement help you to stay strong and keep fighting the good fight, cheering each other onto your God given potential.

I am not the first to have this dream. The founding members of each sorority all dreamed of a friendship so deep and true they were really more like a sisterhood. Your founding members and generations of sorority members ahead of you, all wish for this pure and non-selfish type of friendship.

Each of our sororities were founded on a desire for these true friendships. I believe we are not too far gone. We can get back to the dreams of our founding members to love each other as sisters unselfishly and unconditionally. This starts with you.

I looked up several of your creeds and mottos. Each of your sororities are founded on the high ideals of character and personal development, spurring each other on toward your fullest potential. I wanted to list all of your creeds, but since that would fill a book on it's own, I will highlight just one.

Phi Mu, your creed is beautiful and sums up many of our missions so well. Here is an excerpt:
To walk in the way of honor, guarding the purity of our thoughts and deeds.
Being steadfast in every duty small or large.
Believing that our given word is binding.
Striving to esteem the inner man above culture, wealth or pedigree.
Being honorable, courteous, tender;
Thus being true to the womanhood of honor.
To serve in the light of truth avoiding egotism, narrowness and scorn.
To give freely of our sympathies.
To reverence God as our Maker, striving to serve Him in all things.
To minister to the needy and unfortunate.
To practice day by day love, honor, truth.
Thus keeping true to the meaning, spirit and reality of Phi Mu. [12]

---

[12] http://www.phimu.org/about-us/mission-creed/

I believe sorority women can get back to this dream of sisterhood. I believe you want this. We just need to find our way back. If you want this type of friend, be this type of friend. It could absolutely...

CHANGE
THE
WORLD

"Let us consider how to stir up one another to love and good works." (Hebrews 10:24, ESV).

WORLD CHANGING ACTION STEPS

1. Look up your sorority's creed or motto. What is listed that you want to characterize your life?

2. Do you identify best with Sadie or her sisters? Who in your sorority can encourage you to be the best version of yourself? Who do you know that you could help encourage?

3. Send a text to a sister that needs encouragement, and a sister that inspires you. Set up a coffee date with both.

Chapter 6
Normal is overrated

My mom was a Zeta Tau Alpha and my dad was a Kappa Alpha. I look back at aged pictures of Old South and the composites of hippy haircuts and imagine what is was like when they were twenty. My parents were Greek in the 1970's, forty years ago. I asked them a lot about it. What was the culture like? What was expected of them? What were the parties like? After a lot of funny stories, we concluded that socially speaking, not much has changed. The parties are still constant. Although the pressure on sex, drugs, and rock and roll is more common place (due to social media) the 70's were not exactly wholesome with the whole "free love" (and marijuana) movement.

So here's the thing ladies. Heartbreak and hangovers have been the theme music on Greek row for AT LEAST forty years. FORTY years! Don't you think it's time for something new? Forty plus years of being "typical sorority girls" is simply out of date.

If being normal was getting us somewhere, we would be there by now. It's time to reinvent what it looks like to be a sorority girl.

Chasing Rabbits (for Forty Years)

If you have ever been to a dog race, you have seen the electronic rabbit that is released as "bait" for the dogs to chase, just before the race begins. From puppy-hood, the race dogs are trained to chase the rabbit around the track. They're always taught to run faster, start stronger, and train harder than the other dogs on the track chasing the alluring and seemingly irresistible rabbit that is never realistically within reach.

One day, on a track in Florida, there was a mechanical issue and the rabbit slowed down enough for the dogs to catch it. But the funny thing is, the dogs had no idea what to do when the rabbit was actually within reach. They just stood around barking, jumping, howling, and utterly confused when the allusive rabbit was within snout's reach.

I think this is the same thing that happens in our own lives. We spend our life chasing popularity, beauty, and boys. When these things are within reach, or finally held in our hands, we don't know what to do with ourselves. We think, "is this what I was chasing?"

To add to the illusion, the "rabbits" we as humans chase, are all defined differently. None of us have the same definition of popular, beautiful, and the babe of our dreams. If we ever catch the rabbit we may not even recognize it because we are not even sure what we are chasing.

Celebrity after celebrity seemingly on top of the world is quoted for realizing the "prize" isn't what they thought it would be. All too many have arrived at the top only to be suicidal or addicted.

Why are we chasing?

In my ten plus years of college ministry every young girl's story features the common theme of chasing; chasing popular, chasing pretty, chasing cool and Lord knows chasing boys.

The plot twist happens when people catch their "rabbit" and realize it wasn't even worth it. More often, they get so exhausted running around the track, they are begging for a better way to end this ridiculous race. Sweet friend, there is a better way.

We sell out for so little when God is offering so much.
I love the way CS Lewis describes our chasing, "We are half hearted creatures fooling about with drink and sex and ambition when infinite joy is offered us. Like an ignorant child who wants to go on making mud pies in a slum because they cannot imagine what is meant by a holiday at the sea. We are far too easily pleased"[13]

Why would the most amazing women on the planet settle for being a "typical sorority girl" when infinite joy and the chance to change the world is at your feet?

Shake Up Your "Everyone"

Have you ever thought "everyone is doing it," whatever "it" may be? We all have. We all want to fall in line with our peers. But have you ever thought to define your "everyone."

---

[13]
http://www.goodreads.com/quotes/702-it-would-seem-that-our-lord-finds-our-desires-not

When you live in the same place for a while, you start to think the whole world is just like your "world." I never would have said this out loud but without even realizing it, my logic started to become "if everyone around me acts this way, then this must be how EVERYONE lives."

In my small corner of the globe we never see snow, sweet tea is the drink of choice, and we say "y'all" not "you guys" or "you all." It's "y'all...and that's just how God intended for the phrase to be said. But as it turns out, I know this may be shocking, but the whole world is not this way.

One summer God decided to open up my eyes to how big His world truly is. There is this organization called "Up With People." It's a group of musically talented teens and twenty year olds traveling the world doing service projects and music performances everywhere they go. They rely on host homes in each city to house different members of the crew for the week. Since we have two little girls we figured two big girls would fit right in, so we opened up our home to a nineteen year old from Sweden, and a twenty year old from Vancouver Island, Canada.

The way we dressed, the food we ate, and the things we valued were just so different. One wasn't superior or inferior, just different. Ida, our Swedish daughter for the week, actually celebrated her nineteenth birthday the week she was with us. Wanting to make her feel special at her home away from home, I used the help of Google to give her a Swedish birthday party. The birthday song was in Swedish (thanks to YouTube) and I found all the best Swedish recipes I could find to make her feel at home. To us, this meal was foreign and the happy birthday lyrics were totally unrecognizable. But to her, this was a reminder of what familiar, safe, and normal felt like.

During the week we were also able to meet their friends from Germany, Mexico, New Zealand, and different parts of the U.S. That week felt like we had traveled the globe, yet never left our home. God used that opportunity to completely open my eyes to the great, big, diverse world He has made. People don't look, talk, believe, or even eat the same way at all.

As I write this, it is 8:30 pm on a Sunday night in the summer time. Well, at least it is for me. But also, at this exact same moment, in New Zealand, it is 12:30 pm on Monday afternoon in the winter time! It's like they are living in the future in the opposite season! I am winding down my weekend and they are having their lunch break on Monday! The southern hemisphere has completely opposite seasons as the US. They celebrate Christmas in their warmest months and break out the thick coats in July.

That summer I realized my little definition of "everyone" was embarrassingly microscopic. Our families "world tour" helped me to realize how limited my view had become.

My point is this, our view of "everyone" may be limited. As I said before, show me your friends and I'll show you your future. The people you choose to hang out with have a HUGE influence on your life. Redefine your everyone by going on a mission trip or befriending someone outside of your comfort zone. Reach out to new friends seeking the Lord in collegiate ministries. Eventually your sisters will take notice and want to know more about this Jesus you follow. They will become believers within your sorority and...

CHANGE
THE
WORLD.

The True "Everyone"

This material may come to you as a shocker, but I've done the research and it's true. Despite what you see on TV, the statistics tell us that MORE people are waiting to have sex before marriage, LESS teenagers are getting pregnant, and MORE couples are staying married. [14] You can check my sources; I'm not making this up.

Couples are making wiser choices and your generation wants more than ever, a healthy future for your families.

I also see philanthropy woven into the DNA of your generation. Never has a generation been more eager to serve and make a lasting impact on the world. Your generation is setting precedents in generosity. It is estimated that 85 percent of you give charitably and 70 percent of you volunteer. [15]

Let's be honest, any blockhead can be popular by going to a few

---

[14]

https://consumer.healthday.com/kids-health-information-23/adol escents-and-teen-health-news-719/u-s-teens-waiting-longer-to-h ave-sex-cdc-701550.html

[15]

http://blog.stratuslive.com/generous-generation-millennials-nonp rofits/

parties. But today's world changers are diving into causes that impact their communities and our planet. Hugging the toilet and shacking up with some guy is soooo ten years ago.

Today's sorority women want something better and they are rising up and pouring their energy into causes bigger than themselves.

There is a gradual but undeniable awakening creeping across the horizon of your hearts. I see young people sick of being ordinary, and starving to be extraordinary.

I have a gut feeling that we will look back one day and see this as being the day and age where eighteen to twenty year old's took their dignity back. Start seeing past Friday night and started looking toward big world changing goals.

I love the way Generation Ministries[16] puts it:

Let it be recorded in the history books of Heaven, that the young Christians of this generation responded in radical obedience and dedication to the revelation of the purposes of God for their lifetime. Perhaps we will discover that we came to the Kingdom "for such a time as this!"

16
http://www.youthnow.org/index.php?option=com_content&view=article&id=231&catid=43&Itemid=58

SUCH A TIME AS THIS

You were created for such a time as this, for such a day as this, and to be such a girl as yourself by no accident. You have a glorious invitation to be apart of something so much bigger than you could ever imagine.

A perfect God left his kingdom in heaven. He walked on this earth and had dinner with adulterers and thieves. He invited the "not good enoughs" to be His people and offered the broken hearted a quench for their thirst. But He came for something more than this. A sinful man made a great big divide between us and a great, big, and perfect God. There was no way we could bridge that gap.

Jesus said, "Put the punishment of sin on me," and I'll bridge the gap between a holy God and a sinful man. This God loves all people; this religion is for all people; this was totally brand new.

The moment Jesus died, the Earth shook and the only God in the history of God's to ever rise from the dead walked out of the grave to begin a revolution of love still going on today. Jesus did all of this so a sorority girl 2000 years later would be reading about how she would *change the world.*

Stop running, start being still.
Stop begging, start believing.
Stop yearning, start enjoying.

You're invited to be apart of an adventure so much bigger than what you see around you. An invitation to be part of the biggest motion picture that was or will ever be. The story is already in progress, but it would be so much more exciting with you. The way you're passionate about the things that matter to you, your infectious smile, gentle voice, and every other detail about you can be used for the bigger story.

The story of God is in progress and you're invited to play a supporting role.

Jesus looks at you with love and whispers: I love you too much to see you chase so hard for all of this unattainable happiness that won't last. I see a perfect daughter in you and I want you to be apart of this adventure. Come be apart of something bigger. Come join my story.

WORLD CHANGING ACTION STEPS

1. What are you chasing?

2. Would you know if you found what you are chasing?

3. Have you ever heard the gospel? If you want to read more, start with the book of Matthew in your bible (or get the free bible app).

Chapter 7
Be Brave

Sorority women have more in common than they do different. I have never met you, but I feel confident that you desire a husband one day that will love you unconditionally. I bet you have a hunger to give generously to your community and desire deep and meaningful friendships that spark each other on toward greatness.

But action steps eat good intentions for breakfast.

If I say I want to run a marathon, but never lace up my running shoes would you believe me? If I say I want to lose weight, but keep eating donuts; save money, but keep shopping; learn a new skill, but never sign up for classes, why in the world would you believe me? If I want to travel east, but get on the road to head west, where do you think I will end up?

I can say I want to do something all day long, but the steps I take are what determine where I end up.

The first step is never the biggest, but it will be the hardest. Deciding to take a stand for your faith, suggest a service social, or walking away from an unhealthy relationship will be hard. People may call you crazy but the alternative is they will call you normal. Girlfriend, the majority of my "normal" partying peers have ended up divorced, addicted, and depressed. Normal is highly overrated. It's time to define a new normal on Greek row.

A FEW BRAVE STEPS

At a sorority worship night, I noticed a phenomenon I had seen before, but never fully grasped until that evening. What struck me was the amount of times they had people come to the altar to pray. The music was playing, the sun was set, the stars were rising, and hearts were stirring. And then, a girl would take a few brave steps forward. I can imagine her thinking, "What will people think? Maybe I can just pray where I am. Do I really need to step forward?" But she does. A few seconds (that feel like a few hours) later, her friend comes to pray beside her. And then something amazing happens. The flood gates open up and the altar is full of people praying.

This was interesting, however what I found fascinating is this exact same series of events happened each of the three times there was call for people to pray. It starts as one girl's few brave steps, then one brave friend...and then a movement starts. Every time.

If you want God to do something new, you can't keep doing things the way they have always been done. You've got to push past the fear of the unknown and leave familiarity behind

When one brave girl decides to have fun in a way that's different than puking up Tequila all night, when one brave girl says no to going home with a guy because nothing good will come of it, when one brave girl looks different than her peers, guys take notice, other girls take notice, and changes start to happen.

"Without courage we will simply accumulate a bunch of good ideas and regrets." - Andy Stanley[17]

Fish Casserole

My husband's grandparents had a long standing tradition of making fish casserole on Christmas Eve. It's a labor intensive dish his grandmother would begin making days before they were to eat. Days of soaking, hours of chopping and just the right amount of baking made this dish...well terrible. Everyone pretended to like it because Grandmother slaved in the kitchen for 3 days to make it. Grandmother hated the taste of it herself but always went the extra mile because her family liked it so much (or so she thought).

Finally, one Christmas Eve, my husband who was an outspoken pre-teen at the time exclaimed with a curled up nose "this casserole is gross." The family looked at each other awkwardly around the dining room table until Granddaddy said a hearty "you got that right."

Grandmother was stunned, "I make this every year for all of you." Yet everyone around the table would be happy if the fish casserole became a "Ghost of Christmas Past."

Eventually the conversation turned to laughter and the fish casserole fed the family pets. That was the last year Grandmother had to work so hard for something no one even wanted, but was afraid to tell the

---

17
https://www.goodreads.com/book/show/253303.Next_Generatio
n_Leader

truth.

Hold this thought...

CATHERINE AND MICHELLE

Catherine was tired of living for boys and parties. She had tasted all the world had to offer and it just left her feeling more empty than ever before. The summer after her freshman year she decided to make a commitment to stop drinking. She didn't think any less of her friends who didn't want to make the same commitment, but for her, this was the line in the sand she had to draw in order to make her devotion known to herself and to God.

The first few weeks were easy, but then came the moment of truth. Anytime we step out boldly in our faith, we will be tested; count on it. After all, you can't have a testimony without a test.

Michelle, unbeknownst to her, provided that test. Before Catherine's decision to stop drinking Michelle and Catherine were BPP (best party pals).

They drank each other under the table on any given day that ends in Y. When Catherine kept thinking of reasons not to go drinking with Michelle, Michelle started to take notice. Eventually in friendly confrontation Michelle asked, "Why don't you want to drink with me anymore?"

Catherine stammered with apprehension in her voice said, "I just, I

don't really, I mean I am just more committed to my faith is all."
Catherine was terrified of what her friend would think of her.
Catherine later shared she felt bad that she had an opportunity to say
more, yet was too scared to share her true devotion at that time. God
used that little bit of bravery to spark an interest in Michelle.

Michelle didn't really want to party all that much either. She was
looking for something more than another hangover herself. Michelle
kept asking questions and Catherine eventually invited her to bible
studies instead of the bar.

It wasn't long before Catherine and Ashley became friends who were
much less concerned with the bars and boys, and busy changing the
world instead.

Just like the fish casserole neither of them really liked partying, they
just needed someone brave enough to admit they wanted something
more. Is there any "fish casserole" that you keep eating just because
you think you should? You may be surprised how many people are
relieved when you boldly step out and say you don't like it after all.

"You cannot discover new lands until you have the courage to lose sight
of the shore." -Andre Gide

I think back to all the parties I really didn't want to go to, or the guys I know I really shouldn't have dated all because I *thought* that was what others expected of me. Just like Grandmother assumed everyone wanted fish casserole, sometimes fish casserole is just not all that good in the first place, yet someone has to be brave enough to ask for something different.

One Breath At a Time

We are almost to the end of this book and I haven't even told you that I am also a yoga instructor. I know right! But don't worry, I'm not too much of a hippy and I definitely still take showers…had to clarify that.

I started practicing yoga for strength and flexibility but what I didn't expect was a whole new way of looking at challenges in my life. In the yoga certification process, there is a great deal you learn about breath and the power of the mind. We can get so caught up with 100 thoughts swimming inside our head on a day to day basis.

In yoga class that looks like, "How much longer do we have to hold this?" "My triceps are on fire!" "You want me to put my legs where?"

In college, that looks like, "I know I shouldn't go out with him, but he's cute and I don't want to be single." "Just one more drink won't hurt." "I know I usually make questionable decisions when I hang out with this group but we have fun."

If you are truly wanting to change the world on Greek row you have to decide today, not for the rest of your life, but just today that you will seek the more abundant life as a sorority girl. For you that may mean, not calling him back, signing up for that mission trip, or changing the channel from sex saturated movies.

I pray you make the decision to take tiny steps, one breath at a time, every hour, each day. But decide, just for today, to focus on one positive breath at a time.

World Changing Action Steps

1. Think of a time when someone you know stepped out bravely into a "unpopular" yet respectable opinion. Did you admire her or condone her for it?

2. What is an area of your life where you need to take a few brave steps? Hint...someone reading this needs to break up with a boy!

3. Do you identify with Michelle or Catherine? Maybe neither of you even like "fish casserole" anyway. Think of something new, productive, and world changing you can do with your friends instead.

CHAPTER 8
SOMETHING BIGGER THAN OURSELVES

When I joined a sorority my freshman year of college, it was the first experience I remember realizing I belonged to something bigger than myself. Our chapter president would always say to us at meetings, "You are always wearing your letters." At the time, I didn't think anyone noticed me wearing my letters in my short skirt at the fraternity house until the wee hours of the morning, but they did. My actions no longer affected only me, I now represented a larger organization.

For 18 years, I lived under the false notion that my actions affected me and only me. This concept of belonging to something "bigger than myself" was completely foreign, yet somehow magnetic. As crazy as it sounds, belonging to a sorority was my first taste of experiencing what it's like to belong to the family of God. I represented my sorority, my sisters, and my Jesus when I was serving the community and when I was sloppy drunk making questionable decisions with boys.

What does my sorority stand for? What does my Jesus stand for? Do I care about the reputation of either one?

If you are reading this book, you are more than likely in a sorority which means your decisions always reflect your sisters, your founding members, and your organization as a whole.

If you profess to be a Christian, how do you represent Jesus? You are always wearing His letters. How would He serve, live, and love as a college student?

LIVE LIKE IT

We live in the "information age" where you can access the world wide web from a tiny computer in your back pocket at any point in time. Yet, are we any smarter? When I google "exercise plan" I got 409,000,000 results. We have plenty of ideas and methods of getting fit, yet 68 percent of Americans are overweight or obese. We don't have a lack of information problem, we have a lack of execution problem.

Many of us believe Jesus is real, but very few of us live like it.

"The gospel costs nothing. We cannot buy it or earn it. It can only be received as a free gift, compliments of God's grace. So it costs nothing, but it demands everything. And that is where most of us get stuck — spiritual no-man's-land. We're too Christian to enjoy sin and too sinful to enjoy Christ. We've got just enough Jesus to be informed, but not enough to be transformed."-Mark Batterson [18]

---

[18] https://www.goodreads.com/author/show/66179.Mark_Batterson

Bars, boys, and booze have so been done before. It's time for you to discover the world changer within yourself and let her loose.

The Bible calls it "taking off the old self" and "putting on the new self" (Romans 13:12; Ephesians 4:22-24; Colossians 3:7-10, 14). I don't want to just leave you with some inspiring words, that is a waste of both of our time.

I want you to discover the world changer within yourself and "put on this new self."

In every generation, God has been faithful to bring spiritual awakening to nations. In almost all cases, those movements were most evident among young people.[19]

Sorority women are world changers. You are the trendsetters that can turn any fad into a million-dollar market. Men would do anything it takes to win your heart. You are the women all the guys love! You give generously and serve your community with passion. You share lifelong, deep, and true friendships.

If the parties and the boys didn't deliver what they promised, maybe it's time to try something new. Today is your day to be brave. Everyone is just waiting for someone else to go first. If you are willing to stand up for your faith and start something that matters, those first few steps will be hard, but I can almost guarantee you will have a friend to come beside you and share with you those treasured

---

[19]

http://www.youthnow.org/index.php?option=com_content&view=article&id=231&catid=43&Itemid=58

words, "me too."

I hope I have inspired you to realize the world changing potential you have with your power of influence simply by being a sorority girl. I hope you protect your heart and your body by realizing you are worth more than what the world is teaching you. I pray you want to change your community with service and generous giving. I hope you have friends and become the friend that never settles for normal, because sorority girls are better than normal.

ASHLEY'S DREAM

I will leave you with a true story that is the best evidence I have for the movement I see happening on Greek row.

Minding my own business one day, I was reading "Walls Fall Down For Victory" a bible plan from the bible app[20]. Truth be told, I started the plan about six months prior to this point and never finished it. But, for whatever reason I felt like I should finish up the plan when I came across this verse:

"Now the gates of Jericho were securely barred because of the Israelites. No one went out and no one came in. Then the Lord said to Joshua, 'See, I have delivered Jericho into your hands, along with its king and its fighting men'." (Joshua 6:1-2, NIV)

20

https://www.bible.com/reading-plans/992-walls-fall-down-gods-unusual-plan-for-victory/day/1

The words stood out of my iPhone, but left me bewildered, confused, and a little excited. First of all, what in the ever loving world does this verse even mean?

No one is coming in, no one is coming out. The walls are securely barred and God says (I imagine totally nonchalantly with a little bit of "I mean DUH" to his voice) "I have delivered them."

I knew there was something big there but I didn't know what. I was looking at the commentary and everything. Unable to find any reasonable explanation for this verse I resolved to "I will figure it out later" then went on with my day.

Later that same day, while listening to the audible version of *The Circle Maker*[21] (a book I owe to sending my prayer life through the roof) by Mark Batterson, Batterson mentioned praying over a property for their church that seemed impossible, insurmountable, and just pretty much absurd to even ask for.

While walking prayer circles around the block, Batterson came to the exact same verse!
"The walls were securely barred. No one went out and no one came in. Then the Lord said to Joshua, "See, I have delivered them into your hands"
(Katie paraphrased)

---

[21]

https://www.amazon.com/gp/product/0310330734/ref=as_li_qf_sp_asin_il_tl?ie=UTF8&camp=1789&creative=9325&creativeASIN=0310330734&linkCode=as2&tag=imperpeopl04-20&linkId=45QJ3ORZLHV62DTW

"See, I have already given it to you" God says. "Yes, it looks impossible but you are looking through your eyes, not mine."

Batterson makes the point that what seems impossible to us, is just an invitation for us to pray.
And not just a "wish in the well" type of prayer either, but aligning our prayers with the will of God and *celebrating* what he has already promised!

I almost laughed at the parallels of Greek row where the walls seem so high. The search for significance in sex, drugs, and rock and roll are encouraged in the name of YOLO. Yet, the giving away of our bodies in casual relationships, the hangovers, and the endless search for significance leaves nothing but emptiness...and God says "see I have delivered them."

Call it conviction, call it craziness, but I decided to start praying a circle around Greek row. As in, getting out of my car and being the random "grown up" walking by all the beautiful mansions in prayer. I started praying boldly, in the powerful and matchless name of Jesus that his precious sons and daughters would be taken back into his arms. Rebuking the devil and claiming those big beautiful homes to become houses of worship (all quietly lest I get arrested for people thinking I was drunk).

And guess what... at the end of the row, there was a tarp WALL put up surrounding the perimeter of the most popular fraternity house on row. It's all a "joke" to hide the shenanigans that take place during their philanthropy party week.

A wall surrounding the city....and God says, "I have delivered them."

But wait, there is more. As if I don't already feel the earth shake below my feet. I have a friend named Ashley who was in a sorority the same time I was. We have been friends since college, we got married, had babies, and did life together for ten years. Ashley had a dream that her little family (husband and two kids) would serve as missionaries in Peru. She dreamed of the exact place, the ocean waves, and dozens of vivid details. Today, Ashley and her family live in the mountains of Peru sharing the gospel beside the same white condos and huge waves she distinctly saw in her dream.

Ashley, who was thousands of miles away at this point had no idea about the "walls fall down on Greek row" day I had been praying for my brothers and sisters on row.
Ashley sends me this message,

"Did I ever tell you about the vivid dream I had while in college about Greek row becoming houses of worship? I remember clearly Christ took back His children."

I literally fell to my knees and wept when I got this message. Jesus is taking back his sons and daughters on Greek row my friends. This starts today, with you, one breath at a time. One day at a time living for something bigger than yourself, one social at a time, one break up with a guy that's no good for you at a time. The most incredible trendsetters in the universe are taking their dignity back.

Write it down in the history books, sorority girls are changing the world.

World Changing Action Steps

1. What is one thing in this book you need to re-read right now to truly absorb?

2. What is the first step to changing directions?

3. Choose two friends to discuss your action plan with and ask them to keep you accountable.

Epilogue
Those who have gone before you

When our youngest daughter, Ava, was six, she was terrified to jump off the high dive. She would climb two, maybe three steps up the ladder, then come back down again. This same process continued up and down, over and over again. She never made it even halfway to the top.

Then, her big sister gave it a try. Hannah, who is not quite two years older than her younger sister, bravely took two, then three, then twelve steps up to the top of the high dive. I could see the apprehension in her eyes from the top, but once you're on the top, there is no going back down. Hannah never looked back, she just kept going one step in front of the other until everyone at the pool that day heard the shrill of victory and fear as she leapt into the water.

When she returned to the pool side she was brimming with confidence. She forgot all about the fear and told Ava about the amazing adventure. No more than five minutes later, Ava was jumping with glee into the water from two stories up again and again. My husband and I both had to peel them away from the pool that day. To this day, they still remember that as the best trip to the pool all summer.

Ava was terrified to go up that ladder. In her eyes, it hadn't been done before, it was unfamiliar, and just plain scary. Fear and excitement live in the same place in our brain. The thing that carries you from fear to excitement is courage. Courage often comes from within, but it is so much easier to find that courage when we see someone go first. On the high dive that day, Ava just needed to see someone go first.

We have talked about some inspiring world changing ideas in this book, but sometimes we just need to see someone go first. Below are six sorority women I have had the pleasure to see grow beyond anyone's wildest dream. They are fearless leaders, lovers of Jesus, and live the dream of being a true sister to their friends. These brave women are the ones lighting the way through the narrow and worthwhile journey to beautiful faith in their generation.

Here are their words:

Man oh man, we serve a cool God. The kind of God that sees our flaws, our pimples, our fifty three on our History final and says "you are beautiful". The kind of God that created puppies, carbs, and mountains --yet STILL loves our messy hearts more. I love my sorority and the community it has given me. Although through my sorority I have found friends for life, I have also been reminded God wants us to join His Kingdom-- a unity greater than any letters. So ladies do your squats, wear your letters with joy but never forget our worth is in our creator and our purpose is to serve HIM!

Grace Valentine
www.gracevalentine.org
Founder of The Enough Movement

Something in me told me that I could not take that path that I did in high school. I couldn't go to that dark, cold, and scary place again. I needed to do something different. I needed to FEEL better- physically, spiritually, and emotionally.

So...I ran to Jesus. Not only did I run, but I full on sprinted. During college, I truly found my relationship with Christ, but still felt some uncertainty when it came to trusting Him with all of my being. All I knew is that at this point, I had to hand everything over to Him. I spent my days and nights in prayer, the Word, and in Christian fellowship. I asked Him to help me trust Him because it was hard. I prayed for Him to give me strength and peace and let me tell you... He was so faithful.

Faith Williams

www.christinafaith.blog

I didn't know it at the time, but I looked for my identity in guys. I needed someone to tell me I was beautiful. I needed someone to text me and tell me they loved me. I just love feeling loved. But, as I searched for love in guys, tried living life my way and in my control, and tried satisfying myself with everything this world has to offer, I found out time and time again that it simply does not work.

Abbie Deal

@abbiedeal

I was in the midst of finding my identity in Christ during my freshmen year of college when I was asked to start writing for the Odyssey Online. If I accepted this offer, I would really be putting myself out there by sharing my faith and stories with everyone on the internet! This was scary for me at first, but when I began writing and sharing what God was doing in my life, He began to bless my writing. People began reaching out to me with stories about how they want to grow closer to Jesus, and how they are inspired by my writing. It really humbled me and made me realize that when we take big leaps of faith towards Jesus, He blesses those leaps far more than we can ever hope for. Now, I have my own blog and I love sharing with the internet what God is doing in my life. God has broken down my wall of insecurity, and He has replaced it with vulnerability and trust in Him. Through my writing, I have learned that when we show God our faith and trust in Him, He blesses it beyond measure!
Jenny Way
brokenvesselsforjesus.wordpress.com

I knew God before India, but something shifted in me there. It was like a key to my heart had been unlocked in that city. In India, I made the decision in my heart that God was going to be Lord of everything in my life... Lord of my time, my finances, my relationships, my thought life, and my actions. Every decision I would ever make was to be centered around God. I knew after this trip that the only reason I was alive was to glorify God and invite my brothers and sisters to join me on this vastly exciting journey of leading (serving) people into his heavenly kingdom.
Gabrielle Howard
@Gabbster11 @HowardFashion

Coming into college, I knew that I wanted more for my life. After experiencing all of the shame and regret that came with a past like mine, I was ready to find out who this "Jesus" guy was. I came to college and prayed for a godly group of friends that would lead me and encourage me in my faith and God gave me my sorority. They encouraged me to step out of my little comfortable box and be bold. They prayed for me while I gathered the courage to share my testimony and that's exactly what I did.

I shared my story that consisted of sex, drugs, alcohol, and an abortion. I shared my story so that others would know we CAN experience true freedom. Because of the way God has forgiven me and loved me so generously, that is the only reason I have been able to forgive myself. And none of that would have been able to happen without girls like these. Being a Christian in college seemed boring and hard before I experienced the true joy and freedom that comes with finding your purpose in Jesus.

Carli Salzberg

http://the-lovely-truth.weebly.com/

ABOUT THE AUTHOR

Katie spends her days doing yoga, college ministry, running 5K's with her husband, and playing dress up with her two little girls. Katie also manages to study marketing trends from all aspects for her job in sales. From apparel to media, the evidence is overwhelming every time, sorority girls can change the world.

ACKNOWLEDGMENTS

Alpha Delta Pi, you taught me what it means to exemplify the highest ideals of Christian womanhood. You taught me about sisterhood and gave me some of my best friends. I am forever grateful to be an ADPI.

"Greek world changers," the group we created as more and more girls wanted to hear what it looked like to live a life for Christ and be in a sorority. You guys say I'm the leader, but really you taught me more than I could ever teach you. You are inspiring and amazing women who will totally *change the world*.

Our two little girls. Hannah and Ava, as I write this you are nine and seven. I see you world changers love fiercely and cheer loudly for your sister. You are hilarious, brave, and the kindest little girls I have ever met. I couldn't be more honored to be your Mama.

To Bryan. You always saw a writer in me even when I didn't see it in myself. Thank you for supporting me as this book came together and the wisdom behind many of these truths. Thank you for being the guy who loved me the way Jesus does.

Alia Lewis for editing this book. @ceo_alia
www.clippings.me/alialewis

Ashlyn Cathy for the photo on the front cover @ashlyncathey.photo
http://www.ashlyncatheyphotography.com

Abbie Deal for designing the front cover @abbiedeal

Jesus, lover of my soul, my foundation, my rock and my helper. I can do all things through the one who gives me strength.

Made in the USA
Middletown, DE
14 February 2017